LEADING AND MANAGING POLICY TEAMS

Martin Stanley

Richborne Publishing

ISBN (paperback) 978-1-8384679-4-4
ISBN (eBook) 978-1-8384679-5-1

Published by Richborne Publishing,
68 Richborne Terrace, London SW8 1AX

www.civilservant.org.uk

Cover design by: Ellie Wilkinson of Bluemoon Design Studio

CONTENTS

INTRODUCTION

We have all attended, or will attend, innumerable training programs aimed at improving the way we run our organisations. It took me a long time to realise that the better trainers all said very much the same things, albeit in different ways and using different words. And most of the more valuable lessons applied equally to the private, public and third sectors. Indeed, I have been involved in a number of programs attended by managers from all three sectors, and (after initial mutual suspicion) it has always been the case that they quickly learn that they face very similar problems.

These notes accordingly summarise the key lessons imparted by the best leadership and management trainers. Reading these notes will not exempt you from attending such training, but will hopefully help you make sense of it. They will also help you identify the rubbish advice that is offered by the less effective trainers (and your less effective senior managers).

But please bear in mind that even these notes are to some extent idealistic and cannot reflect the unrelenting pace at which modern managers are expected to work.

Good managers are supposed to be reflective, organised, rational and plan-oriented. Real managers' work is characterised by brevity, variety and discontinuity. A study of CEOs found that half of managers' activities lasted less than nine minutes. A study of British middle and top managers found that they worked uninterrupted for more than 30 minutes only about once every two days.

Similarly, good managers are trained to empower and delegate. They are told to be like good conductors: they orchestrate everything in advance and then monitor the results. In practice, of course, managers have a number of regular duties that only they can perform. It is a natural part of a manager's job to meet important customers/stakeholders, attend retirement parties, meet government officials (or vice versa), and so on. These duties cannot be delegated.

So, although the following advice is sound, it cannot help you find the right mixture of leadership, planning, empowerment, change management and so on that will fit your particular circumstances. But it will certainly help reduce the number of mistakes that you make.

Speaking of which, management is a bit like driving. It's all about taking decisions, often every few seconds – how to react, what tone to adopt, when to change the subject. However hard we try, some of our judgements will be wrong, but hopefully inconsequentially so. Good managers, like good drivers, simply make fewer faulty decisions than others. Firm but fair managers can apologise and move on, for their colleagues recognise their worth and forgive the occasional blemish. Unpopular, unfair managers find that their mistakes are leapt upon as evidence of their inadequacy.

LEADERSHIP

Leadership is about who you are.

Management is about what you do.

Michael Bichard, a former Permanent Secretary, draws a clear distinction between managers and leaders: *Managers who control their organisations effectively may enable them to survive. But it is the leaders who create a sense of purpose and direction, and who analyse, anticipate and inspire.*

Strong leadership is essential if your team is to be innovative, efficient and successful. And yet one of the minor mysteries of the modern world is why there are so few effective leaders – in both the public and private sectors – when there is so much advice available in so many different books and courses. Indeed, they all say pretty much the same sort of thing which is that:

- **Leaders are different** from their followers. They are not their 'buddies'.
- **They tell their people that they are different, and they behave as if they are different.**
- Effective leaders are **authentic**. (Staff will quickly spot imposters.)
- Staff expect their leaders to be **courageous** and **empathetic.**
- Above all, good leaders can always answer the following questions from anyone at any time:
  - Where are we going?

- Why are we going there?
- How will we get there?

In a little more detail, effective leaders often

- have a *remorseless* iron determination to make things happen;
- have an unshakeable inner conviction;
- keep things simple;
- are a little theatrical;
- are authoritative and respected;
- are *committed* to their team;
- accept blame;
- are *honest*
- are physically and mentally resilient, and
- take risks.

I would only add that my own observation, for what it is worth, is that too few public sector leaders are sufficiently *remorseless, committed, and honest.* Let me explain what I mean ...

Remorselessness

The first and most important characteristic of a leader is remorselessness. This takes two forms.

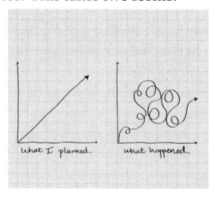

what I planned.　　what happened.

First, leaders feel no remorse when they make mistakes, when things do not go according to plan, or when some innovation fails to work. They recognise that they are dealing with humans, not machines, and human behaviour is highly unpredictable. Remorse and guilt are understandable, but quite unnecessary, even if something does not work in the way you expected.

Second, leaders are remorseless (in the sense of relentless) because they know that every improvement will take two or three times as long as they expect it to. But they don't let this stop them. Instead, they keep plugging away and eventually they and their teams achieve levels of performance that others can only dream of.

Commitment

Different situations call for different styles of leadership. Decisions sometimes need to be made very quickly and obeyed without question. But leaders nowadays almost always need the consent of those that they lead. Management consultants Kouzes and Posner describe leadership as 'a reciprocal relationship between those who choose to lead and those who decide to follow,'

Modern leaders therefore need to be a cross between an old-fashioned captain of a ship and someone who is running for office. It follows that newly appointed leaders should go out of their way to get themselves elected – i.e. respected by their teams – in the first few days after their appointment. This simple fact does not seem to be understood by many colleagues.

If you are to be elected leader then you must commit to the team, with all its strengths and weaknesses. This is particularly important in the civil service if only because you are unlikely to be around long enough to replace them. And the civil service is anyway so large that, by definition, it has to employ a cross-section of the population. Of course, you do not need put up with mediocrity or laziness. But you cannot insist on surrounding yourself with energetic geniuses. Your task is to get the best out of those who work for you, without forever wishing yourself somewhere else.

How do you show your commitment? You should:

- be very visible, in particular by walking about;
- set a good example, including by complying with rules and standards that have been set for your team;
- champion the team e.g. by defending them against unfair criticism, but also
- respond to fair criticism, whether of you or your team, in particular by putting matters right and by ensuring that the problem does not recur.

More generally, good managers and leaders tend to spend more time with their direct reports than do other managers - and bad managers spend very little time with their staff. This all seems very obvious but a middle manager friend of mine told me that three weeks passed before her newly appointed Senior Civil Servant (Deputy Director) boss got round to meeting her, and she had yet to meet her Director after six months in the job. So some colleagues still have something to learn about visibility, commitment and leadership.

Honesty

According to Lucy Kellaway, writing in *the Financial Times*, a good leader knows exactly when to be straight, when to be economical with the truth, when to lay it on with a trowel, and when to dissemble. This is absolutely right, but most of us spend too much time dissembling and too little time being honest with our staff. We treat them as grown-ups when discussing their work, but not necessarily when it comes to talking about their own jobs. If we don't know something, or we are unsure, or we have made a mistake, we should tell them.

In particular, we have to be honest in making it clear to staff that they are employed for no other reason than to help the leader achieve his or her objectives. However much they enjoy working together, the team must be directed to achieving a common goal. Everyone is then much better directed and motivated. Those who skirt round this fundamental truth simply waste time and create confused expectations.

Effective leaders also give clear and honest feedback to their staff – not all the time, but frequently enough to change behaviour. Any sustained failure to give honest feedback to colleagues – and of course we have all failed to some extent, and regretted it – can only end in disappointment, confusion and demoralisation. Honest appraisal is also a necessary companion to empowerment. Once the manager has defined the job that is to be done, they should aim to keep out of the way and let their staff do what is expected of them, subject, of course, to informal and formal reviews to ensure that the work stays on track.

But ...

The problem with my pen picture of an effective leader is that it equally well describes Winston Churchill and Adolf Hitler; Nelson Mandela and Stalin. So some leaders are qualitatively better than others. What marks them out? It is clearly the **values** that they promote, and the boundaries that they set:-

VALUES

Different organisations inevitably have somewhat different values, though new leaders could do much worse than adapt those of Netflix, summarised at Annex A.

Values are of little use if they are merely written down – and swiftly ignored or forgotten. Good leaders lead by example, rather than by coercion. I like the quote attributed to St Francis of Assisi: *"Preach the Gospel at all times and when necessary use words"*.

Bad leaders, in contrast:

- talk a good game, but have no impact
- make everything look great while they are there - but everything falls apart after they leave
- improve financial performance whilst having no impact on the organisation's other results - such as exam performance in schools or medical outcomes in hospitals
- are decisive and incisive - achieving 'quick wins' but neglecting the investment and other factors that lead to long term success.

The best leaders carry out a difficult balancing act. On the one hand they are obsessive about setting the correct boundaries and establishing the right culture. On the other hand, they empower and support. Those who get it right can usually then stand back and watch their team achieve surprising results.

(Andrew Gordon believes that Nelson's most essential contribution to British naval mastery was as a trainer of Admiral Collingwood and others. "His greatest gift of leadership was to raise his juniors above the need of supervision.")

The best leaders know that they are most likely to achieve 80% of their impact in 20% of their time. It is of course difficult to identify that 20%, but don't fool yourself into thinking that very long hours will make a great deal of difference. They are much more likely to blunt your effectiveness.

Contrary to popular belief, you don't need to be tall and handsome to be seen by others as a natural leader. But strength, or resilience, certainly helps. Most of us would, for instance, follow this man almost anywhere.

Morgan Stanley's Head of Security, Rick Rescoria, is a great leadership role model. Almost all their 2,700 employees made it out of the South Tower on 9/11 because he had previously insisted on regular evacuation drills. When the planes struck, he overrode the Post Authority's instruction to 'stay put' and started evacuating immediately. Because of the drills, everyone knew what to do. Bravely, tragically,

Mr Rescoria was last seen heading back up the tower to see if he had left anyone behind.

CHRONIC UNEASE

One essential trait, in today's increasingly complex world, is chronic unease; the best leaders are constantly on the alert for vulnerabilities in their organisation and systems.

They in particular challenge *'Let's Do It!'* recommendations – these are, by definition, the ones that could possibly lead to accidents and disasters. Alert leaders look for weak signals that something is not right, that something could go wrong. These can always be found (in hindsight) after major disasters. And they reward those who respond properly to such signals.

Good leaders do not cease to listen if they are deluged by complaints. They instead listen carefully and try to identify the underlying causes of the complaints. They are particularly concerned to identify systemic problems that might have large scale or devastating consequences.

The attitude of the local authority and the Tenant Management Organisation were obvious examples of failure to listen to concerns in the period before the Grenfell Tower fire which killed 72 people. But two civil service examples came to mind just as this booklet was going to print.

A 2021 National Audit Office investigation into the underpayment of state pension found that the Department for Work & Pensions had probably underpaid 134,000 pensioners over £1 billion in State Pension.

This was because the pension rules were only fully understood by a small group of specialists. The under-payments were therefore due to repeated human error over many years, some level of which was almost inevitable given the system's high degree of manual review and complex rules. Front-line staff found instructions difficult to use and lacked training on complex cases.

The NAO also found that the department had not implemented their previous recommendation to measure detected underpayments and did not assess whether individual detected under-or-over payments had a systemic cause that might indicate a wider error.

And

A Prisons and Probation Ombudsman report into the death of a baby in a prison found that the mother should have been checked by a nurse every morning, afternoon and evening and a minimum of twice during the night, but this did not happen. The mother rang her cell bell at 8.07pm that evening and asked for a nurse. No nurse was called. She pressed her cell bell again at 8.32pm. The call was not answered on the house block and was diverted to the permanently staffed communications room. At 8.45pm the call was connected and immediately disconnected. Ms A did not press her cell bell again.

At 8.21am next day, two prisoners alerted wing staff to blood in Ms A's cell. An officer investigated and discovered that Ms A had given birth during the night. Nurses attempted to resuscitate Baby A and called an ambulance. At 9.03am, paramedics confirmed Baby A had died.

Information sharing within the prison and health agencies was poor and the approach to managing the mother was uncoordinated. No one responsible for her care had a full history of her pregnancy. None of the multiple record systems involved spoke to each other, none of the separate records contained sufficient information on their own for proper oversight and no one person had access to them all.

There might be something to be said in defence of those responsible for pension and prison policy, but the inescapable conclusion seems to be that senior officials in both departments were unforgivably oblivious to, or unconcerned about, serious and persistent problems which led to the above disasters.

MANAGEMENT

Leadership and management are inseparable – the two sides of the same coin – and yet quite different. Leadership is about who you are. Management is about what you do. Management is the process of achieving your aims by getting the most of out the resources at your disposal, and in particular getting the most out of your team.

It is perhaps worth stressing up front that managers need to be ready to be unpopular. You and your staff may be friendly and enjoy each other's company, but you cannot be friends.

Management can be emotionally draining because it involves telling people what to do, and what not to do. You should not be unpleasant to your colleagues. You should listen to them and - if you agree with them - you should be their advocate. But you should not, at the end of the day, care whether they like you. You must be prepared to be an authority figure, because you are one.

Most management processes involve the following:

- Establish the identity of your customer: the person (a Minister?) that you are trying to please – not necessarily (or usually) the person who is managing you.
- Establish (with your customer) your **aims** and **objectives**. How will the customer know whether

you have done what (s)he wanted?

- Choose an appropriate **strategy** – best thought of as the route that will most efficiently get you to your objective – and then develop a more detailed plan, at least for the first few stages.
- Identify what resources you will need and, in particular ...
- Create and motivate an appropriate team.
- Measure progress towards the objective, using milestones as necessary.
- Revise the strategy and plan as and when necessary.

Let's now look at Strategy, Aims and Objectives in more detail.

STRATEGY

'Tactics without strategy is the noise before defeat'. – Sun Tzu

Vague aims, vision statements and the rest seldom assist either managers or those they manage. "We are going to be the best in the world at what we do" is not a strategy. It is a vague ambition. And words like *synergy* and *customer-centric* add nothing to the sum of human knowledge.

Your organisation may have its own strategy or vision. Your job is to translate it into something that makes sense, and that inspires you and the people working with you. Do not hesitate to re-frame a vague corporate strategy to make it more relevant to what you do.

Strategy requires making choices. The best strategies are those that say what you are not going to do. If you can't do this then you will have little more than a meaningless jumble of words.

A good strategy will generally include:

1. A diagnosis that defines the challenge that you face.
2. A guiding approach or route map which will help you deal with the challenge.
3. A set of coherent actions and objectives consistent with '1' and '2'.

AIMS AND OBJECTIVES

Many organisations set far too many aims and objectives, so that priorities are unclear. Indeed, few of us can cope with more than three tiers of Aims, Objectives and Targets. And whilst an *objective* of the Permanent Secretary of the Home Office might be to cut crime, or keep it to a certain figure, this would become part of the *aim* of more junior officials who might be responsible for the Police Pension Scheme. The important thing is that those in charge of the pension scheme should know that it needs to be so designed that it will attract and retain high calibre police officers (and that is their quantifiable objective) in order that those officers might in turn cut crime.

If anyone has difficulty in accepting worthwhile objectives, as distinct from day to day targets and activities, it is helpful to ask them what would change, or how they and their team would be missed, if they did not exist. Alternatively, the line manager should help them complete the sentence beginning *"You will be a success if you ..."*. It always makes both of them think!

And take care! Objectives are powerful things, especially when linked (as they should be) to appraisal. Get them wrong and your whole organisation will go off in the wrong direction. Take particular care if you are tempted to define your objectives in monetary terms. This approach can sometimes be very effective. Equally, it can turn you all into novice accountants, quite oblivious to your wider or longer-term responsibilities. See also the advice on measurement in the section on planning, below.

The aims and objectives of individual staff members should if possible be 'SMART', i.e. Specific, Measurable, Agreed, Realistic and Time-dependent. And they should be kept **simple** and **relevant** to the person who owns them.

Although the job/responsibility plan should emphasise the importance of achieving worthwhile objectives, rather than the ability to demonstrate a range of grade-related skills or behaviour, it should also make it clear what levels of skill, effort and achievement represent satisfactory performance. This will help those who wish to show that their performance has been much better than satisfactory. It can also be useful to deploy the concept of 'breakthrough performance' when trying to explain the difference between what is in the civil service generally known as 'Box 2' rather than 'Box 3' (i.e. satisfactory) performance.

Although I always write the first draft of the person's objectives, the document obviously has to be shown in draft to the person being managed. In particular, I have often found it helpful to ask colleagues to say, in effect, what they offer to do by way of satisfactory performance. This can help dispel unreal expectations that satisfactory performance somehow deserves of an exceptional report. Indeed, I take the firm view that Box 2 breakthrough performance cannot be recognised in the absence of a clear agreement between manager and managed which specifies the level of performance that has been exceeded.

For Civil Servants only:-

Civil servants have traditionally drafted their own objectives or job plan. This approach was unfortunately enshrined in official guidance when objectives-setting was first introduced in 1986. Why 'unfortunately'? It is surely axiomatic that managers should take responsibility for defining what jobs they want done, what sort of person they want to do them and what standard of performance is expected. This should be clearly set out in a document which draws as necessary on the department's and directorate's written objectives, and should in the first instance be drafted by the manager, not the managed. After all, who else but the manager can in the first instance say why a particular individual is employed within their team?

And too many civil servants default to job descriptions that are all about what people do ('I give policy advice...', 'I manage...') rather than what they are trying to achieve. The usual response, of course, is that things like the health of an industry, or of the population, are dependent upon so many variables that it is positively unfair to credit any one civil servant with their improvement. There is of course some truth in this, but it is also true that a great deal of effort will be wasted unless it is directed towards an identifiable (even if distant) objective. Also, the adoption of challenging and worthwhile objectives leads quickly to innovation, team working and other good practices.

But note that it is genuinely difficult for some **senior officials** to be explicit about their and hence their Ministers' objectives, for Ministers will often *either* refuse to be specific (for fear of being seen to fail) *or* will announce some dramatic objective which, within days, appears imprecise or unattainable. Therefore, although most senior officials, from Permanent Secretary down, nowadays have written objectives, they are often almost meaningless.

If you don't already have a favourite standard *Personal Responsibility Plan* (or similar), you may find the one at Annex B helpful.

PLANNING AND MEASUREMENT

Having set your objectives, you must now plan how you will get there.

Planning is of course an unnatural process. It is, after all, much more fun to do something. And the other nice thing about not planning is that failure comes as a complete surprise rather than being preceded by a period of worry and depression. But experienced managers know that planning is (a) relatively simple (which is perhaps another reason why it does not appeal to many civil servants) and (b) an indispensable precursor to success. The main thing, therefore, is to do it! But when you do it, these are the key points that need to be borne in mind.

- Keep it simple;
- Focus on results, i.e. what is to be achieved;
- Ensure individual responsibility for all members of the team, preferably by managing through a structured breakdown of the project into constituent parts which are the responsibility of named individuals;
- Communicate, and in particular clearly communicate both objectives and progress both within and outside the team;

- Monitor progress both carefully and frequently.

Much of the above implies measurement. This lies at the heart of effective management, whether of the policy process or of anything else. We all know – though we often forget – that 'you cannot manage what you do not measure'. Another version of this saying is that 'If you measure it, you change it' - which leads to the conclusion that you should 'Make the important measurable, not the measurable important.' This really is the key to success in all your endeavours, and time spent on unmeasured activity is the most likely time that is being wasted.

However, ... at the risk of repeating what I have said earlier, don't let your measurements so dominate your life that they distract you from achieving your objectives. As the old adage has it: 'Weighing the pig will not make it fatter!'".

Do not be tempted to organise long and complicated staff or customer surveys. Five questions, with answers on a 10-point scale, will often do quite nicely. Customers, for instance, might be asked about the extent to which your team understand their needs, helps them achieve results, handles their matters efficiently, keeps them informed, and uses initiative on their behalf.

BUILDING SUCCESSFUL TEAMS

Much has been written about how to create and build successful teams, but Judy Foster (author of *Building Effective Social Network Teams*) summarised it very well when she stressed that there are five key enabling factors:

1. Coherent policies
2. Effective professional development
3. A sense of autonomy: the ability to innovate in response to customers' needs
4. Sound support structures, including well-run and genuinely participative management meetings
5. Sufficient mental space to be able to process difficult emotional situations, see clearly and think creatively. This includes supportive supervision provided by more experienced colleagues.

Judy's research showed that mental space is particularly vital – and in short supply in some of the social work teams that she studied. I suspect that much the same can be said of many civil service teams who spend too much time attending inefficient meetings and/or fire-fighting in response to short-term pressures, and taking far too little time to think clearly and creatively.

Does Morale Matter?

Morale, just like happiness, can be surprisingly elusive. It is a great mistake to try directly to improve morale. Good morale comes naturally to any well-managed team, and never comes to a team that is poorly led, lacks clear objectives, is poorly trained or lacks good honest communication. So, if you are lead and manage well, high morale will inevitably follow, however difficult the surrounding circumstances.

Do also bear in mind that morale will inevitably dip during a period of rapid change. The team does not at first realise that it needs to change. (This state is sometimes unkindly referred to as *'unconscious incompetence'*.) Once it faces up to its problems then confidence and morale will inevitably decline (*'conscious incompetence'*). It will then begin to do better, although perhaps rather self-consciously (*'conscious competence'*) and finally morale will rise rapidly once the new way of working has become second nature (*'unconscious competence'*). It is then the job of the leader to ensure that this state is maintained for as long as possible, through seeking continuous improvement, so that the team does not slip back into unconscious incompetence.

Establishing a Great Culture

Leaders set the tone of the organisation – even in small but important ways. For instance, I hope that any visitor to my office will find that we are open, informal and hospitable. We feel that it makes a real difference if we are friendly and polite to each other, and offer refreshments and other courtesies to visitors. We in particular welcome the opportunity to talk about our work, and our approach to our work, and welcome visits from colleagues from embassies, from industrialists, from students and from teachers.

I also expect everyone to recognise their responsibility for the safety, health and well-being of themselves and all their colleagues. We take the alarm bells seriously, even if we suspect that they are a false alarm. We take seriously all reports of sexual harassment, racial or sexual discrimination, or bullying. We give unquestioning support to colleagues who express concern about safety, harassment or discrimination. Above all, we do not ask colleagues to work so hard that they become stressed or over-tired. This is not only unethical, but it leads to mistakes and misjudgements – which in turn create more pressure.

Next, I encourage everyone to be **customer-focused**, where our customers are defined as the immediate beneficiaries of particular pieces of work. If you are preparing a briefing, your customer is the person who will use it. If you are organising a meeting, your customers will be those who attend the meeting. Our customers should be the sole and decisive judge of the quality of our work. The test is not whether we think that our work meets the requirements of the customer, but whether the customer is satisfied.

This implies measurement (again!). You cannot tell whether your customer is satisfied unless you have asked him or her in a structured way. It should become second nature that your plans and your day-to-day work are driven by the expressed needs of your customers.

Measurement in turn drives **continuous improvement**. You and your team should constantly be looking out for ways – usually quite small in themselves – in which you could improve the satisfaction of the customer, or do the job more efficiently or effectively. The cumulative effort of many small improvements can be very noticeable indeed. Conversely, a cumulative failure to improve will eventually and inevitably lead to your customers feeling dissatisfied with the service that you are providing. It follows that imitation is a virtue. If you hear of a good idea, or see something working well, you should not hesitate to copy it so as to improve the service that you are providing to your customers. And if you run out of ideas for improvements, you should benchmark your team against another team or organisation. You will probably be surprised at what you find.

Continuous improvement in turn requires a **no fault culture**. We assume that everyone is trying to do a good job, within the limits of their skills, training and experience.

Management gurus often say that 'customers' complaints are jewels to be treasured'. This is a bit over the top for most of us, but it is certainly true that complaints should never be ignored, and a single complaint often represents the tip of an iceberg of unvoiced dissatisfaction. Quality conscious organisations are therefore usually obsessive about investigating and resolving customer complaints, whether from internal or external customers. And complaints should never be used as a stick with which to beat your staff or other colleagues. If mistakes are made, or if quality standards are not met, then the person involved should be given clearer instructions or better training, or attention must be given to the process that they were carrying out, or to whether they are in an appropriate job. (This judgement should not be arrived at lightly, but neither should it be ducked. If necessary, the person must be moved to a job that they can do.)

There is also plenty of research that shows that high reliability organisations encourage and reward error-reporting. Best-performing nursing units, for instance, have been found to have higher detected rates for adverse drug events than did lower performing units . This counter-intuitive finding almost certainly meant that a climate of openness made nurses more willing to admit errors – and learn from them – not that there were in fact more errors. A good reporting culture is of course nowadays central to the safety of the airline and some other industries.

Staff Surveys

It is important to know what your staff think about their jobs, including how well they are being managed. Some staff surveys are extremely lengthy and hence unfocussed. I prefer to use the more simple survey at Annex C.

It is important, of course, to arrange for the answers to be collated by an independent person or organisation so that anonymity can be preserved.

Setting Boundaries

It is vitally important that leaders should establish the ethical, financial, legal and other boundaries within which their colleagues should work. Problems (and sometimes severe problems) arise when these are not explicit or, even worse, when senior managers appear themselves not to respect those boundaries. It is particularly important that civil servants should operate within the ethical, financial and legal boundaries laid down by Parliament and summarised in my book *How to be a Civil Servant.*

Many boundaries are cultural, rather than ethical, in the sense that leaders are responsible for establishing the parameters within which staff deal with each other, with customers, with work pressures and so on. It is worth noting that some staff will constantly test your boundaries and force your intervention when the boundaries are likely to be breached. They will accuse you of micro-management. Other staff will respect your boundaries, and get on with their jobs with very little intervention from yourself. They may as a result worry that you are not interested in them or their work area. It is therefore important that you explain your approach, and reassure those who think you have taken empowerment just a little too far.

Empowerment

Empowerment is often confused with delegation. Delegation often means no more than that the delegate is simply told what to do and how to do it. Empowerment is better because it allows the colleague to choose how best to achieve his or her objectives and targets. Leaders don't delegate. They empower.

Empowered staff must of course work within constraints laid down by their managers, including appropriate professional standards, standard procedures, quality standards and financial constraints. You should help them gain experience by empowering them, monitoring their performance and acting to relax the constraints - by giving them great financial freedom for instance, or freedom to innovate - as soon as you can.

For Civil Servants only:-

Submissions, draft letters etc. should be prepared by the person, however junior, best equipped to prepare a first draft. If the issue is not novel or contentious, and the person is appropriately experienced and trained, then there should be no need for the work to be countersigned by anyone else. Two heads are however better than one if an issue is novel or contentious. A senior colleague who countersigns work in these circumstances should concentrate on the substance of the work, and the way it will appear to Ministers or the recipients of letters etc. They should pay relatively little attention to the detail, style or grammar of the work.

Work should also be countersigned if the action officer is being trained or gaining experience. It is helpful in these circumstances if the countersigning officer pays attention both to the substance of the work and to the detail, style and grammar. The objective of this intervention should, however, be to train the colleague so that countersignature is in due course not necessary.

RECRUITMENT

Recruitment has to be taken enormously seriously. Get it wrong and you'll have nightmare months or years trying to correct your error. Get it right and your job becomes much easier.

But it is very hard to get recruitment right, partly because we are often reluctant to spell out exactly what attributes we don't want, as well as what we do want. There is, for instance, plenty of room for shy, retiring, academic individuals in some policy-making teams, but many policy jobs require staff to be friendly, self-starting, clear communicators and so on. These attributes need if necessary to be spelt out and appraised, or else you will end up appointing an unemployable genius - great at completing crosswords but quite incapable of making decisions or managing fellow humans with all their faults and frailties.

It must be recognised, too, that recruitment is inevitably risky because you don't have a lot of time to get to know all the candidates before appointment. You must therefore be ready to accept that some appointments will not work, through no fault on the part of you or the appointee.

Here are some thoughts that might help you cut the error rate.

General Advice

- You do not want 'the best' person for the job. You

want the right person – one who fits the job re-
quirement, whose strengths are those you need,
and whose weaknesses won't be shown up.

- Take care to ensure that the job description and
person specification are comprehensive. If you
need the appointee to be friendly, approachable
and flexible, then this needs to be spelt out in
advance. Equally, if the job can be filled by a
shy, backroom sort of person, then other attributes will need to be stressed. You may find Nancy
Holloway's questions useful in framing both the
person specification and subsequent lines of questioning – see Annex D.

- Do encourage genuine diversity. Your approach
should <u>not</u> be *"Come in and we'll show you how to
be like us"*. It should be *"Come in … and now we are
a new organisation"*. Even today, women seeking
promotion often feel the need to be 'the right sort
of chap' in both background and behaviour. This
needs to stop.

- Similarly, do not demand sophisticated drafting
skills from everyone. There is a marked waste of
talent in many government departments because
good managers, good networkers (especially with
those in industry), good 'deliverers', and many
professionals are deemed unsuited to working
closely with Ministers.

- Take care not to be fooled by embellished and
exaggerated CVs, and do take oral references in
advance of discussion/interview. Having learned
from bitter experience, I would not appoint to
a middle-ranking or senior position without taking a quite deep prior reference. Some candidates

cannot supply these for good reasons, but others cannot provide them because they have been dismissed for incompetence or worse. It is seldom worth taking the risk.

- Equally, do take a moment to think about the motivation of the referee. Some managers are trying to get rid of poor quality staff, and hope you will end up holding this particular damaged parcel. And some will bad mouth staff who do not fit their particular mould, although you might rather welcome a recruit who is a little out of the ordinary.
- Do not downplay the difficult aspects of the job for which you are recruiting. Many public-facing positions, for instance, and jobs in Ministers' offices, are very stressful, as are jobs (such as some regulatory jobs) whose outputs are subject to intense scrutiny, including by the courts. The need for these positions to be filled by robust personalities must be spelt out to all candidates as it is no kindness to them (or you) if they are appointed to a job in which they cannot succeed.
- Unless you feel that the candidate will be uncomfortable working for you, do not hesitate to recruit people who are more experienced than you - or have useful different experience.
- If the candidate needs a particular skill, make sure you thoroughly test them to ensure they have it.
- But don't require academic qualifications unless absolutely necessary. An experienced person who opted out of post-16 or higher education will often out-perform those who studied longer.
- You sometimes need to find someone who will

shake up an organisation. Private sector friends of mine - who often serve together on interview panels - ask each other "Is (s)he life threatening?" ! (The right answer is "yes'.)

- Psychometric testing is almost always a waste of time.

And there was this sensible advice from Head of the Civil Service, Mark Sedwill, speaking in 2019:

> Of course, people have to get jobs on a meritocratic basis, but you will often find at the end of an appointment process ... that if it comes down to the last two people, you can't really say 'this one's better than this one'."

> At that point, a leader should consider who is "a better fit right now". That might mean when an agency's leader moves on, for example, their replacement should have a different leadership style because the agency has evolved.

> [And remember that] ... often the people who are working for you are better at what they're doing than you would be.

By the way – never, ever, let your HR department make decisions for you – even (indeed especially) at the preliminary sift stage. They will too readily sift out that unusual, left-field but exciting candidate, maybe without exactly the right qualifications, that would transform your team.

Interviews

- Interviews should be conversations, not interrogations. Respond to, and if necessary challenge, what the candidate says. Make sure you understand why they have given an apparently odd answer to one of your questions.

· Do not put too much weight on performance in the traditional 45-minute interview. Some candidates think much more quickly than others, and/or are more able to express their thoughts orally. These may be important attributes - but in many cases you will be better off appointing a deeper thinker, or someone who takes time to order their thoughts in way that allows them to communicate more clearly - especially in writing.

· It is much better, therefore, to arrange for short-listed candidates to have two discussions (not 'interviews') with two different halves of a four-person recruitment panel. These feel more relaxing for the candidate and can allow issues to be explored in greater depth. This facilitates a much deeper investigation of the candidates' interests, character, strengths and weaknesses. This may seem time consuming, but it is a lot less time consuming than dealing with the aftermath of a less than optimal appointment.

· It is best to rank candidates in advance of final discussion/interview based on a careful (and sceptical/evidence based) review of their achievements in previous jobs. The discussions can then be used to test the accuracy of the ranking rather than as an event on which the whole process hinges.

· There is no 'equal opportunities' need to ask all candidates the same questions. Interviews should be tailored so as to tests the candidate's likely strengths and weaknesses. Although the job specification is the same for all candidates, their experience and apparent strengths will vary, so your questions need to vary if you are to accurately assess their suitability for the job.

· If an experienced manager with a good track record has a strong (and likely negative) hunch about a candidate, listen to that person and explore the concern in depth.

(Don't forget that civil servants must be appointed on merit through fair and open competition.)

And please try to avoid silly application forms. Can it be true (I fear it was) that judges - applying for high office - must provide an example of how they behaved with integrity?

Remember, too, that recruitment needs to be followed by effective, targeted **induction**. This is too often neglected, especially in the case of senior appointments; this is one of the reasons why I created my Understanding the Civil Service and Understand Regulation websites.

(It is particularly important that new entrants to the civil service are introduced to the Civil Service Code, and come to understand its importance and implications. There should be no question of local mission statements or departmental core values overriding the provisions of the code.)

PERFORMANCE MANAGEMENT & APPRAISAL

Informal appraisal is very important. Blanchard & Spencer's *The One Minute Manager* suggests that managers should give immediate feedback whenever they see good or bad work. In the real world, unfortunately, too many managers give immediate feedback that is either always positive (and therefore dishonest) or always negative (which is debilitating). Colleagues quickly learn to appreciate the honesty of the few managers who give both sorts of feedback.

Negative feedback should be delivered carefully, taking great account of your relationship with the person whose performance you hope to improve. If you don't know them too well, perhaps because they haven't worked for you for very long, you should generally – if possible - start by offering a compliment about work done well, or simply an acknowledgement that you haven't yet seen much of their work but ... something concerns you. Some experienced managers recommend *bookending* or *sandwich criticism* – both starting and finishing with something positive. The reason for both these approaches is that, if you start with a negative, your colleague's defences will go up and they won't properly hear what you are saying.

But the positives in the above approaches can too often be seen as insincere window dressing so – if you can – try instead to engage in a tactful, honest and mature conversation which shows that you are sensitive to the other person's feelings and genuinely want them to change/improve.

Sadly, however, our lives are too often dominated by ...

Formal Appraisal Systems

It has been known for decades that formal appraisal can do more harm than good. Academic researchers in this area generally conclude that ratings don't reveal much about the ratee, but instead reveals rather a lot about the rater.

Douglas McGregor pointed out as long ago as 1957 that managers are uncomfortable when they are put in the position of 'playing God'. Here are a couple of extracts from his *Harvard Business Review* article.

There is always some discomfort involved in telling a subordinate he is not doing well. The individual who is "coasting" during the few years prior to retirement after serving his company competently for many years presents a special dilemma to the boss who is preparing to interview him.

Nor does a shift to a form of group appraisal solve the problem. Though the group method tends to have greater validity and, properly administered, can equalize varying standards of judgment, it does not ease the difficulty inherent in the interview. In fact, the superior's discomfort is often intensified when he must base his interview on the results of a *group discussion* of the subordinate's worth. Even if the final judgments have been his, he is not free to discuss the things said by others which may have influenced him.

The conventional approach, unless handled with consummate skill and delicacy, constitutes something dangerously close to a violation of the integrity of the personality. Managers are uncomfortable when they are put in the position of "playing God." The respect we hold for the inherent value of the individual leaves us distressed when we must take responsibility for judging the personal worth of a fellow man. Yet the conventional approach to performance appraisal forces us not only to make such judgments and to see them acted upon but also to communicate them to those we have judged. Small wonder we resist!

The modern emphasis upon the manager as a leader who strives to *help* his subordinates achieve both their own and the company's objectives is hardly consistent with the judicial role demanded by most appraisal plans. If the manager must put on his judicial hat occasionally, he does it reluctantly and with understandable qualms. Under such conditions, it is unlikely that the subordinate will be any happier with the results than will the boss. It will not be surprising, either, if he fails to recognize that he has been told where he stands.

Of course, managers cannot escape making judgments about subordinates. Without such evaluations, salary and promotion policies cannot be administered sensibly. But are subordinates like products on an assembly line, to be accepted or rejected as a result of an inspection process?

(A later Harvard Business Review article, along the same lines, is at Annex E.)

Commenting as recently as 2019, Twitter's *Flip Chart Rick* pointed out:-

> 'Much of the design and re-design of performance management processes in the intervening 6 decades has been about trying to manage our discomfort. The more process and bureaucracy we put around it, the more we hope to shield ourselves from the emotional pain Management fads and fashions come and go. Ten ratings or five? Or four? Competencies, capabilities, objectives, frameworks, all trying to do one thing. Make this whole thing look objective so we can hide our discomfort. None of it has really worked, though it has cost a lot!'

Nevertheless ...

Despite what is said above, most readers will be forced to deliver or receive formal appraisals is delivered within a structured system over which they have only limited control. Here is some advice which might help limit the damage.

First, it is important to remember that **we all have different mixtures of strengths, experiences and weaknesses**. Managers should not make a big deal if the appraisal system forces them to mention weaknesses that may be quite irrelevant in the current job. Equally, the person being appraised should not get too upset if a weakness is pointed out- or misunderstood - in an otherwise positive appraisal.

Second, it is often the case that **a single weakness can be a major problem**, and this needs to be spelt out and addressed. Too many senior officials have reached their current positions despite being inexperienced or poor managers, simply because they score well when it comes to analytical ability and the like. It would be much better for all concerned if such weaknesses were addressed early in such careers, and regarded as an absolute bar to further progress.

Third, the **formal annual appraisal** is essentially one-way communication. The process might begin with self-appraisal (although I have my doubts about the effectiveness of this approach) but it is essentially an opportunity for the appraiser to be honest about how the other person has appeared to them over the preceding period. The person being appraised might well feel that the appraiser is wrong, and it is fine to discuss this, but if the manager is unconvinced then it shouldn't lead to lengthy debate. Any difference of opinion can be resolved over the coming months as the staff member demonstrates their true ability to their manager. There should be no question of the appraisal being 'agreed' by the person being appraised, or subject to any form of appeal.

It is sensible, however, to show draft appraisals to the person on whom you are reporting, for you might well have forgotten some achievement, or you might have expressed something in an upsetting way. But the report should nevertheless remain your honest assessment of the other person, in comparison to other civil servants.

Fourth, appraisals should usually lead to **action**, whether by way of improved communication between manager and managed, or changes to objectives and expectations, or further training and development.

Fifth, **keep it simple!** No-one remembers the detail of an appraisal more than a few hours after reading it. When I ran a small department, we categorised staff as very effective, effective or not effective, and this worked very well, especially if allowance was explicitly made for those who were in the process of gaining experience.

Finally, it is better if appraisals are supplemented by 'upward feedback' or even **'360-degree feedback'**. There are several good systems that facilitate these processes but it must be stressed that they need to be carefully managed if they are not to do more harm than good. They should certainly not amount to 'upward appraisal'. Managers should want to know what messages their staff believe that they are receiving, in particular through the managers' behaviour. But it is not for staff to tell managers whether the messages are appropriate, or whether the manager is regarded as doing a good job. There may be some saints who would respond enthusiastically to criticism from inexperienced staff, but I fear that I and many others are not amongst them – at least until I have worked with my critics for a good long time.

See also, Annex F, for advice on how to deal with accusations of **bullying and harassment**, including those that arise during performance management

FURTHER READING

As well as the books mentioned above, I recommend Tony Rossiter's book *Management Basics* as a very readable combination of plain common sense and the kind of unofficial tips that are rarely written down but which go a long way towards making a decent and effective manager.

I also strongly recommend Lucy Kellaway's entertaining demolition of the worst management fads. You can find it here:- https://www.civilservant.org.uk/library/ The_Best_of_Lucy_Kellaway.pdf

There is much good sense to be found - albeit indirectly - in cartoons such as *Dilbert* and *Clare in the Community*. I am particularly grateful to Harry Venning for allowing me to reproduce the cartoon at Annex F. It, and many others, can be found in *The Clare in the Community Collection* which covers Clare's 25 years in *the Guardian*.

My own book and long reads are listed at Annex G.

ANNEXES

There is much to be said for using, and if necessary adapting, leadership and management material which has been prepared by previous generations. So I have collected together the following material, much of which i have in turn plagiarised from my predecessors. You are therefore very welcome to copy and use it without attribution.

Annex A   Netflix's Values

Annex B   A Personal Responsibility Plan

Annex C   A Staff Survey

Annex D   Interview Questions

Annex E   Staff Appraisal - A Critique

Annex F   Bullying, Harassment and Performance
Management

Annex G   My Other Writing

A. NETFLIX'S VALUES

<u>Judgement</u>

- You make wise decisions (people, technical, business, and creative) despite ambiguity
- You identify root causes, and get beyond treating symptoms
- You think strategically, and can articulate what you are, and are not, trying to do
- You smartly separate what must be done well now, and what can be improved later

<u>Communication</u>

- You listen well, instead of reacting fast, and so can better understand
- You are concise and articulate in speech and writing
- You treat people with respect independent of their status or disagreement with you
- You maintain calm poise in stressful situations

<u>Impact</u>

- You accomplish amazing amounts of important work
- You demonstrate consistently strong performances so colleagues can rely upon you
- You focus on great results rather than on process
- You exhibit bias-to-action, and avoid analysis-

paralysis

Curiosity

- You learn rapidly and eagerly
- You seek to understand our strategy, market, customers, and suppliers
- You are broadly knowledgeable about business, technology, and entertainment
- You contribute effectively outside of your speciality

Innovation

- You re-conceptualize issues to discover practical solutions to hard problems
- You challenge prevailing assumptions when warranted, and suggest better approaches
- You create new ideas that prove useful
- You keep us nimble by minimizing complexity and finding time to simplify

Courage

- You say what you think even if it is controversial
- You make tough decisions without agonizing
- You take smart risks
- You question actions inconsistent with our values

Passion

- You inspire others with your thirst for excellence
- You care intensely about Netflix's success
- You celebrate wins
- You are tenacious

Honesty

- You are known for candor and directness
- You are non-political when you disagree with others
- You only say things about fellow employees you

will say to their face
- You are quick to admit mistakes

Selflessness

- You seek what is best for Netflix, rather than best for yourself or your group
- You are ego-less when searching for the best ideas
- You make time to help colleagues
- You share information openly and proactively

B. SAMPLE PERSONAL RESPONSIBILITY PLAN

To ....

This minute summarises what I would like you to do whilst you are working in the Regulatory Impact Unit over the next year or so. It also summarises certain of my commitments to you.

Your Objectives

You lead a team whose main aims are:

1.   To ensure that the Task Force provides timely and effective advice to the Prime Minister, to the Minister for the Cabinet Office and to his departmental colleagues:

- about the principles which should be applied to regulations,
- about new regulatory proposals, and
- about existing regulations, focusing on the scope for removal or simplification.

2.   To ensure that Departmental Ministers take full account of Better Regulation Task Force advice, and that significant failures to reconcile the views of the Task Force and those of a department are reported to the Minister for the Cabinet Office and if necessary to the Prime Minister.

3.   To ensure the trouble-free Third Session enactment of legislation which will improve the effectiveness of the Deregulation & Contracting Out Act 1994.

Your principal objectives are summarised in "RIU's Aims and Objectives".

Working Style

We are all under a great deal of pressure, especially from No.10. Our central and high profile role, the status of the Task Force - and its individual members - and the nature of our Ministerial clients, means that we cannot cut corners, relax our professional standards or provide an inadequate service whether to internal or external customers. Equally, however, we are expected to work efficiently and innovatively, and to respond quickly to requests and questions. I therefore expect you:

a)   to concentrate on important and worthwhile objectives, ruthlessly to prune or eliminate work on issues which are peripheral to your main objectives listed above, and to eliminate unnecessary record-keeping, consultation etc.

b)   to manage your team so that they too work in a very focused, innovative, efficient and effective way in support of your aims and objectives. You will in particular need to ensure that they have the right experience and appropriate and timely training, including coaching.

c)   to ensure that your secretarial and administrative support team work in an efficient mutually-sup- portive way and are not asked to carry out tasks which add little or no value to the work of your directorate. As rule of thumb, I would not expect the size of this team to exceed 20% of the size of the whole of your directorate.

d)   to take controlled risks. I expect that both you and your team will make mistakes, and I will defend you when you do so.

Meeting the Needs of your Customers

Everyone in your team should be trying to "hand it on with pride": i.e. ensure that their immediate customer, whether a member of the task Force, a colleague, a Minister or a member of the public, is satisfied with the work or service that they receive.

This particularly applies to the Task Force members - and especially [the Chairman]. In order to achieve this, you need to set a good example yourself. You should also have simple but effective systems which ascertain the needs of your customers - and in particular the Task Force - and measure their satisfaction with the performance of your team.

Professional Standards

The essence of your professional skill is that you should be able to get things done whilst respecting the ethical and other constraints within which civil servants must work.

The standards to which I expect you to work are summarised in a set of notes which you have seen, and you should immediately let me know if you find any difficulty in following the guidance in that document. I would particularly draw your attention to:

a)   Your duty to Parliament, which means that you have to take particular care with the taxpayer's money. You and your team should only authorise expenditure and payments when you are wholly satisfied that you have the power to do so, that the expenditure represents good value for money, and that all the necessary notifications, checks etc have been undertaken.

b)   Your duty to Ministers, which means that you must provide them with reliable and unbiased support and advice whether in person or in the form of submissions, briefing, Parliamentary Answers or speeches. Your professional advice, and your decisions, must be based on a sound understanding of the facts and circumstances applicable to the issues for which you are responsible.

c)   Your duty to treat all members of the public, and all your colleagues within the public service, with equal respect and consideration.

Keeping me informed

The basic rule is that I am interested in what you achieve, not how you achieve it. I therefore do not want to see copies of most correspondence etc.* *However:-* in order that I can relax in the knowledge that all is going well, I need to know that you are providing a good service to our principal customers. I also need to know what is going on so that I do not appear too ignorant when I meet these customers. You should therefore ensure that I am kept in touch with progress on major and high profile issues, and also told about and copied into all but the most routine dealings with the Prime Minister, all Cabinet Ministers including of course the MCO, all other Cabinet Office Ministers, Parliament (as represented by Parliamentary Branch), [the Cabinet Secretary], [the Permanent Secretary] and all Directors.

*[*This will need to be amended if the post-holder is inexperienced, newly promoted, or new to the subject area. It may then be necessary for the line manager temporarily to see/check more of the post-holder's work.]*

Assessing Your Performance

It is already clear that you are a very capable and energetic Senior Civil Servant who should have no difficulty in getting "3+"s.

So how do you get a **Box 2**? In short, you have to *surprise* me by achieving more than the basic performance is required by this PRP. This is sometimes referred to as "breakthrough performance". In practice, this often involves a combination of achieving more than is required by certain aims, and demonstrating surprising quality whilst achieving other aims.

I believe that you have plenty of scope to do this, particularly by helping the Task Force to become a force to be reckoned with. This will mean helping the Task Force to write reports etc. which are powerful and compelling, and helping them gain the confidence to press much harder than in the past for their recommendations to be accepted by departmental Ministers and officials. They must also work much more effectively with the MCO and No.10.

Other areas where you should be able to shine include:
- improving the flow of information to the Task Force so that they feel better plugged into the work of the wider unit,
- adding value to the work of ...'s team, and, in particular,
- getting the Task Force to work harder and more effectively on the deregulation agenda, and, of course
- getting the Bill through smoothly and without significant controversy, given that it will attract a good deal of attention.

My Commitment to You

I for my part undertake:

- to be open and fair in my dealings with you;
- to give you clear authority and responsibility for running your team;
- to delegate effectively and to the maximum possible extent, and to involve myself in operational matters only where I can add significant value;
- to ensure that you have the resources needed to achieve the objectives set out in this PRP;
- to support you when necessary in your dealings with Ministers and with other internal and external customers (e.g. in resisting unreasonable demands and in dealing with unjustified criticism);
- to assess your performance objectively,

> openly and fairly on the basis of this PRP; and
> to recognise and reward good performance;
> · to give you the opportunity to develop and
> broaden your skills so that you can improve
> your performance in your present post as
> well as prepare to fill quite different jobs, in-
> cluding jobs of a higher weighting. (Your
> Personal Development Plan is summarised
> below.)

Personal Development

Example:-

[It is helpful that you have had a varied career and I am not currently aware of any pressing training or development needs, other than to continue to learn on this challenging and exciting job. However, you should look out for other opportunities to undertake interesting activities, even if not directly relevant to your present job. And in due course, maybe about a year from now, think you should look out for an opportunity to go to a management school or similar, mainly to give yourself some time out, and an opportunity to review your skill set alongside others of your generation, including non-civil servants.]

MARTIN STANLEY

C. EXAMPLE OF A GOOD STAFF SURVEY

Please indicate, by circling the appropriate figure, the extent to which you are content with the five features of your job.

1. Clarity of Objectives

I have no idea of the purpose of my job, or what I am expected to achieve.		I fully understand the purpose of my job, and what I am expected to achieve.

0 1 2 3 4 5 6 7 8 9 10

2. Appropriate Quality of Work

I spend all my time doing work which either does not interest or challenge me, or which is too difficult for		I spend all my time doing work which interests and challenges me, and is not too difficult for me.

me.		

0 1 2 3 4 5 6 7 8 9 10

3. Training and Experience

I have had no training or experience which has prepared me to do my job effectively.		I have had the right training and experience to prepare me to do my job effectively.

0 1 2 3 4 5 6 7 8 9 10

4. Appropriate volume of work

I always have far too little work to do.	I have just the right amount of work to do.	I always have far too much work to do.

-10 -9 -8 -7 -6 -5 -4 -3 -2 -1 0 1 2 3 4 5 6 7 8 9 10

5. Assessment and Feedback

I have no idea how well my managers and colleagues believe that I am performing in this job.		I fully understand how well my managers and colleagues believe that I am performing in this job.

0 1 2 3 4 5 6 7 8 9 10

D. SOME GOOD INTERVIEW QUESTIONS

Many job advertisements require candidates to be good team-workers, have good communication and interpersonal skills etc. etc. But what does this mean in practice? The late Nancy Holloway offered the following definitions which others might find both helpful in designing questions, and also thought-provoking.

Teamwork/flexibility

- Are you a friendly and approachable colleague and will you get on with the team you are in and the wider culture, including working with other teams without any problem, and freely sharing information?

- Will you be happy to have new bits of work thrown at you/work to a different boss from time to time/work in project management style in different teams with people from around office?

Communication/interpersonal skills

- Can you write well?

- Can you speak coherently and (for more senior posts) compellingly when briefing or presenting information?

- Can you organise your thoughts and present them in concise manner that you're your message across in plain English?
- Do you relate well to other humans (as opposed to machines etc.) and are you able to strike the right note with external stakeholders in meetings/phone etc.?
- Can you read others well, and respond appropriately?

Management/organisational skills

- Can you manage other people without either diving in too deeply and doing their work for them or leaving them without guidance?
- Are you selfish about claiming credit or can you coach and help others develop?
- Can you work in a no-blame culture but still get people to perform?
- Can you organise your own work/work to deadlines?
- Can you juggle conflicting priorities?
- Can you use IT well and manage paperwork?

Analytical skills/ability to deal with complex information and data/solution focused

- Are you able to stand back from an issue, pick out important issues in problem you're dealing with, find solutions/ways forward?
- Are you able to relate your issues to those others within the office are dealing with and to the bigger picture for the organisation as a whole including corporate aims and objectives?

- Are you able to sift through large quantities of information or data and quickly see problem areas?
- Are you able to present a coherent and well-argued solution/way forward?

Self-starter/ability to work on own initiative/ multi-tasker

- Are you the sort of person that doesn't sit and wait for someone to tell you what to do, has ideas, is quick to learn, make suggestions for improvements, and get on with work on your own without constant supervision and advice?
- Are you able to think on your feet and respond to changing situations?
- Are you able to juggle a number of things at once and be able to work out which is most important/ urgent?
- Do you know when to ask for help and from whom?

Representational skills [if appropriate]

- Will you be able to represent the organisation in public or at meetings with stakeholders?
- Will you be able to demonstrate an understanding of issues around office and an ability to relate them coherently to others?
- Are you able to hold your own when briefing senior people?

Regulatory aptitude [if appropriate]

- Are you comfortable with both collaborating and confronting people/issues with external stakeholders, and do you know when to choose the correct one of these approaches?

- Do you feel comfortable with economic concepts and working with economists?

- Do you feel comfortable with working within a legal framework which controls the limits of what you can do and working with lawyers?

- Can you see around corners and anticipate trouble before it happens?

- Do you have a questioning mind that doesn't just accept things you're told at face value?

- Can you negotiate with difficult people?

E. STAFF APPRAISAL

Harvard Business Review Feb 2015

How good a rater do you think you are? If you were my manager and you watched my performance for an entire year, how accurate do you think your ratings of me would be on attributes such as my "promotability" or "potential?" How about more specific attributes such as my customer focus or my learning agility? Do you think that you're one of those people who, with enough time spent observing me, could reliably rate these aspects of my performance on a 1-to-5 scale? And how about the people around you – your peers, direct reports, or your boss? Do you think that with enough training they could become reliable raters of you?

These are critically important questions, because in the grand majority of organizations we operate as though the answer to all of them is *yes, with enough training and time, people can become reliable raters of other people.* And on this answer we have constructed our entire edifice of HR systems and processes. When we ask your boss to rate you on "potential" and to put this rating into a nine-box performance-potential grid, we do it because we assume that your boss's rating is a valid measure of your "potential"— something we can then compare to his (and other managers') ratings of your peers' "potential" and decide which of you should be promoted.

Likewise, when, as part of your performance appraisal, we

ask your boss to rate you on the organization's required competencies, we do it because of our belief that these ratings reliably reveal how well you are actually doing on these competencies. The competency gaps your boss identifies then become the basis for your Individual Development Plan for next year. The same applies to the widespread use of 360 degree surveys. We use these surveys because we believe that other people's ratings of you will reveal something real about you, something that can be reliably identified, and then improved.

Unfortunately, we are mistaken. The research record reveals that neither you nor any of your peers are reliable raters of anyone. And as a result, virtually all of our people data is fatally flawed.

Over the last fifteen years a significant body of research has demonstrated that each of us is a disturbingly unreliable rater of other people's performance. The effect that ruins our ability to rate others has a name: *the Idiosyncratic Rater Effect*, which tells us that my rating of you on a quality such as "potential" is driven not by who *you* are, but instead by *my* own idiosyncrasies—how I define "potential," how much of it I think *I* have, how tough a rater I usually am. This effect is resilient — no amount of training seems able to lessen it. And it is large — on average, 61% of my rating of you is a reflection of me.

In other words, when I rate you, on anything, my rating reveals to the world far more about me than it does about you. In the world of psychometrics this effect has been well documented. The first large study was published in 1998 in *Personnel Psychology;* there was a second study published in the *Journal of Applied Psychology* in 2000; and a third confirmatory analysis appeared in 2010, again in *Personnel Psychology*. In each of the separate studies, the approach was the same: first ask peers, direct reports, and bosses to rate managers on a number of different performance competencies; and then examine the ratings (more than half a million of them across the three studies) to see what explained why the managers received the ratings they did. They found that more than half of the variation in a manager's ratings could be explained by the unique rating patterns of the individual doing the rating— in the first study it was 71%, the second 58%, the third 55%.

No other factor in these studies — not the manager's overall performance, not the source of the rating — explained more than 20% of the variance. Bottom line: when we look at a rating we think it reveals something about the ratee, but it doesn't, not really. Instead it reveals a lot about the rater.

Despite the repeated documentation of the Idiosyncratic Rater Effect in academic journals, in the world of business we appear unaware of it. Certainly we have yet to grapple with what this effect does to our people practices. Look closely and you realize that it will cause us to dismantle and rebuild virtually all of them.

Fueled by our belief in people as reliable raters, we take their ratings — of performance, of potential, of competencies — and we use them to decide who gets trained on which skill, who gets promoted to which role, who gets paid which level of bonus, and even how our people strategy aligns to our business strategy. All of these decisions are based on the belief these ratings actually reflect the people being rated. After all, if we didn't believe that, if we thought for one minute that these ratings might be invalid, then we would have to question everything we do to and for our people. How we train, deploy, promote, pay, and reward our people, all of it would be suspect.

And yet, is this really a surprise? You're sitting in a year-end meeting discussing a person and you look at their overall performance rating, and their ratings on various competencies, and you think to yourself "Really? Is this person really a '5' on strategic thinking? Says who – and what did they mean by 'strategic thinking' anyway?" You look at the behavioral definitions of strategic thinking and you see that a "5" means that the person displayed strategic thinking "constantly" whereas a "4" is only "frequently" but still, you ask yourself, "How much weight should I really put on one manager's ability to parse the difference between 'constantly' and 'frequently'? Maybe this '5' isn't really a '5'. Maybe this rating isn't real."

And so perhaps you begin to suspect that your people data can't be trusted. If so, these last fifteen years have proven you right. Your suspicions are well founded. And this finding must give us all pause. It means that all of the data we use to decide who should get promoted is bad data; that all of the performance appraisal data we use to determine people's bonus pay is imprecise; and that the links we try to show between our people strategy and our business strategy — expressed in various competency models — are spurious. It means that, when it comes to our people within our organizations, we are all functionally blind. And it's the most dangerous sort of blindness, because we are unaware of it. We think we can see.

There are solutions, I'm sure. But I think, before we can even consider those, we must first stop, take stock, and admit to ourselves that the systems we currently use to reveal our people only obscure them. This admission will challenge us. We will have to redesign almost our entire suite of talent management practices. Many of our comfortable rituals — the year-end performance review, the nine-box grid, the consensus meeting, our use of 360's — will be forever changed. For those of us who want HR to be known as a purveyor of good data — data on which you can actually run a business — these changes cannot come soon enough.

———————————

Marcus Buckingham provides performance management tools and training to organizations. He is the author of several best-selling books and the forthcoming StandOut 2.0: Assess Your Strengths, Find Your Edge, Win at Work (Harvard Business Review Press).

———————————

F. BULLYING, HARASSMENT & PERFORMANCE MANAGEMENT

Dame Laura Cox QC published a report in 2018 into bullying and harassment in the Palace of Westminster. It contained some very helpful general advice and definitions, especially for managers (a) who receive complaints of bullying, or (b) who are concerned that they may be accused of bullying when trying to improve the performance of their staff. The following text is taken almost verbatim from Dame Laura's report.

What is Bullying?

The report contained two useful definitions of bullying:

- Behaviour that cannot be objectively justified by a reasonable code of conduct, and whose likely or actual cumulative effect is to threaten, undermine, constrain, humiliate or harm another person or their property, reputation, self-esteem, self-confidence or ability to perform.

- Offensive, intimidating, malicious or insulting behaviour, an abuse or misuse of power through means intended to undermine, humiliate, denigrate or injure the recipient.

The report noted that bullying or harassment:

- may be by an individual (perhaps by someone in a position of authority such as a manager or supervisor) or involve groups of people.
- may be obvious or it may be insidious.
- may be persistent or an isolated incident.
- can also occur in written communications, by phone or through email, not just face to face.

Whatever form it takes, bullying is unwarranted and unwelcome to the individual.

Performance Management

Staff who are facing criticism of their performance may feel that they are being bullied by their critical manager. The report offered this sensible advice:

When introducing new standards of performance, a good manager will usually involve all the members of the team in agreeing them, rather than seek to impose them without discussion and with accompanying threats of disciplinary action if they are not met.

Positive contributions and improvements in performance will be monitored, acknowledged and rewarded openly, rather than dealt with arbitrarily, involving obvious acts of favouritism, or just ignored altogether.

A failure by someone to achieve the required standards will be dealt with initially as a performance-improvement issue, the employee being treated with civility throughout and with the provision of appropriate support, rather than pressure to conform being exerted using sarcasm, ridicule, threats or humiliation, often in the presence of others in the team.

An under-performing employee should know from the start that their performance is under investigation, and why, rather than learning only after the event that it has been under investigation for some time, and that disciplinary action is now imminent.

Comment: This advice is sensible but I would add that I think it unfortunate that HR professionals generally refer to formal performance management warnings etc. as 'disciplinary action'. The word 'discipline' implies serious fault and should, I think, be reserved for genuinely bad behaviour. Under-performing staff need to have their performance managed – if necessary to the point of dismissal - but they will often be in the wrong job for their skills and experience. I don't think that they should be 'disciplined'.

The Need for Full Records

The report noted that: Patterns of behaviour are extremely important in tackling bullying. It is always right to consider whether the "perpetrator" was under acute pressure and just having a bad day, for example, and whether this was just an isolated outburst with no lasting effects and the behaviour was out of character, or whether such incidents had happened before.

It is therefore important for organisations to maintain reliable records and to log reported incidents and their outcomes accurately, and to have systems in place to enable patterns to be picked up and their historical and systemic significance understood.

G. ALSO BY MARTIN STANLEY

If you join my free subscription service at http://
eepurl.com/hF489L I will send you free PDF versions of future publications.

Book

How to be a Civil Servant was first published in 2000 and is now in its fourth edition.

Long Reads

Mt first long read - **Speaking Truth to Power** - was published in 2021.

This long read - **Leading and Managing Policy Teams** was published in September 2021.

It will be followed by **Understanding Organisational Behaviour** in October 2021.

Future titles might include *Civil Service Reform, Effective Regulation, Effective Consultation, Handling Crises, and The Ethics of Large Organisations*

Websites

Understanding the Civil Service (www.civilservant.org.uk) is very popular, achieving 500,000 page views a year. It demystifies the working practices of those UK civil servants who work closely with ministers, and describes the ethical and other constraints within which they work.

Understanding Regulation (www.regulation.org.uk) (70,000 page views a year) aims to demystify and explain the rather more specialised, but increasingly important, world of regulation.

Notes

Printed in Great Britain
by Amazon

67308465R00047